Little Book of
WOODEN BOWLS

Little Book of
WOODEN BOWLS

WOOD-TURNED BOWLS CRAFTED BY MASTER ARTISTS FROM AROUND THE WORLD

Kevin Wallace and Terry Martin

FOX CHAPEL
PUBLISHING

© 2019 Fox Chapel Publishing Company, Inc., 903 Square Street, Mount Joy, PA 17552.

Little Book of Wooden Bowls contains content from *New Masters of Woodturning*, first published in 2008 by Fox Chapel Publishing Company, Inc.

ISBN 978-1-56523-997-5

The Cataloging-in-Publication Data is on file with the Library of Congress.

To learn more about the other great books from Fox Chapel Publishing, or to find a retailer near you, call toll-free 800-457-9112 or visit us at *www. FoxChapelPublishing.com.*

We are always looking for talented authors. To submit an idea, please send a brief inquiry to acquisitions@foxchapelpublishing.com.

Printed in Singapore
First printing

CONTENTS

INTRODUCTION

Woodturning in the 21st Century

During the 1960s and 1970s, turned wooden bowls first came to be considered as objects of contemplation rather than simply of function. An art-like market gradually developed among collectors who considered such bowls too beautiful to use. Turners of vision started to ignore tradition, and to make pieces that broke many of the old "rules" of the craft. It was a quiet revolution, but a strangely disconnected one, because many participants had no idea what the others were doing. If anyone read about woodturning, it would have been in books emphasizing the trade values of techniques, not of innovative shapes or aesthetics.

In 1976, the American writer Dona Z. Meilach first documented the work for what it was—the beginning of a new art movement. In her book, *Creating Small Wood Objects as Functional Sculpture*, Meilach assembled much previously scattered history and put it into a larger context.

She was probably the first person to describe turning as "sculptural" and to refer to turners as "artists." Meilach also introduced people who would shape the new field such as Melvin Lindquist, Bob Stocksdale, and Stephen Hogbin. Meilach's work alerted many artists to the fact that there were others like them, and also inspired many newcomers to join the movement.

During the 1970s and into the 1980s, the then-new *Fine Woodworking* magazine published a series of articles that reached an enormous audience around the world and changed the future of turning forever. The series included stories on turning delicate bowls of exotic timber by Bob Stocksdale; heavily spalted wood, previously unheard of, by Mark Lindquist; green turning, a technique practiced by turners for hundreds of years, by Alan Stirt; inlaid wood with hi-tech finishes by Giles Gilson, and, most significant of all, a 1979 article by David Ellsworth on hollow turning. Ellsworth laid down his challenge to

Ron Fleming, *Yama Yuri*, 2006. Basswood, acrylics; 36" high x 17" diameter. Fleming created the turned vase as a vehicle for the painted lilies, which are life-size. He says, "I had to reinvent the air-brush process to be able to apply frisket on a curved surface. There's more than 400 hours in it."

the turning world: "Bowl turning is one of the oldest crafts. It is also among the least developed as a contemporary art form." Ellsworth was good at explaining the technical aspects of his work—lathe specifications, speed, tools—but he also introduced language and a philosophy that had never before been heard in relation to turning: "The concentration involves all senses equally, and the center of focus is transferred to the tip of the tool." It was heady stuff, just right for the times, and it hit the mark in a culture ready for rule-breakers.

In 1980, Dale Nish of Provo, Utah, published the milestone book *Artistic Woodturning*. Nish showed foresight when he put the word "artistic" on the cover and he introduced ideas that profoundly influenced turners around the world. Nish spoke of paying "tribute to nature's designs," and of making the most of faults and damage in wood. Nish was one of the first to chronicle the changing ways turners were using wood, and their new approaches to displaying its beauty.

A New Collector

The new work attracted a new kind of collector, people who not only fell in love with the lure of wood, but also believed the leading woodturners could become the new art stars. It was not to be the case. If the new turning heroes became famous, it was not in the broader art field, but among the legion of aspiring turners with lathes in their garages who sought to create similar work. The amateur artisans formed a new market for tools and hardware, and for a time each new turning idea generated a new line of equipment. From sophisticated hollowing systems to ever-larger lathes, vast numbers of tools were manufactured and sold to the burgeoning amateur market. As a result, a thin and difficult-to-navigate line developed between amateurs who were able to create technically proficient work, largely by imitating or taking classes from their heroes, and those who had a distinctly original aesthetic vision that propelled the field forward.

Very early on, a small group of woodturners emerged as the collectible masters. The group included James Prestini, Bob Stocksdale, Melvin and Mark Lindquist, Rude Osolnik, and Ed Moulthrop. As the field expanded during the 1980s and 1990s, new artists entered the gallery system, among them such innovators as Todd Hoyer, Stoney Lamar, Michael Peterson, Giles Gilson, John Jordan, Mike Scott, and Michelle Holzapfel. The infusion created challenges for new collectors and curators, who had to navigate a scene where accomplished artists exhibited alongside emergent novices. The early success of the true innovators suggested originality was the key to sales, so the new generation began to create ever more unusual and technically complex work. At the same time, some who had already made their mark by creating original work seemed condemned to repeat their ideas incessantly, to satisfy the desire of collectors to own a signature piece.

Round No More

Woodturning is unlike other traditional woodcrafts. In carving, furniture making, and carpentry, one takes pains to hold the wood still so it can be worked by moving tools. In woodturning, the lathe rotates the wood itself against a hand-guided tool. The inversion has two valuable consequences: much turned work can be completed right on the lathe with no additional processing, and woodturning offers a very quick path from fallen tree to finished object. It also brings a limitation formerly seen as inviolate: turned work is round.

Much of the wood art in this book inverts those truisms: the lathe is merely the beginning, with additional off-lathe processing to come. It is not at all quick, and it no longer has to be round.

Most of the early innovators made their work entirely on the lathe and the artists in the book generally started out doing the same. Most of them spent many years mastering the traditional skills of turning before feeling the need to add other techniques. Many don't use the lathe nearly as much now, and some struggle with whether they are "turners" at all. A piece of wood might spend a very brief time on the lathe, followed by months of reworking, sometimes removing or concealing any evidence it was initially turned. The trend in turned wood art now is to carve, burn, paint, recut, and rework pieces.

Once woodturning was valued for how quickly and inexpensively it could be done, but now artists boast of how many months they spend reworking a piece after turning it. However, many say their work is still "defined by the lathe" and most admit to a deep-seated love of the very ancient craft of turning. It is true that even when a piece has been reworked extensively, its beginnings as a round and symmetrical shape still will show through—its lines are too powerful to entirely disguise. The artists' loyalty to the lathe may seem surprising, however, because it is the work they do after turning that makes their work distinctly their own.

The beauty of wood is what attracts many artists in the first place, and much early work celebrates it. It is about the wood's appearance, smell, grain, texture, and links with the natural world. In the early days, a clever use of wood grain was enough to claim artistry. Even now, when artists may obscure the wood by texturing, burning, and painting, it still has appeal in its warmth, heft, and vitality.

For many of the artists in this book, their immediate environment is another important part of who they are and what they create, and pursuing a solitary craft with an uncertain income is their method for being able to live in places they love.

Astonishing New Techniques

For a long time, many who were promoting wood art liked to compare it to ceramics and art glass. They were looking for a vocabulary to help build credibility in the top-end market. In reality, contemporary wood art uses techniques as exciting as anything being done in other fields. If anyone doubts turned wood art is now as much about carving, texturing, sanding, and painting, they only have to look at the astonishing work represented in these pages.

While turned wood art has its roots in utility, today's artists often encounter a prejudice against function. Galleries, collectors, and museum curators tend to frown upon production work and functional bowls, suggesting those woodturners will not be accepted as "serious artists." However, many woodturners continue to produce functional multiples as a means of supporting their families and because they simply enjoy the work.

From ancient and humble beginnings, woodturning has been transformed into an art form for the twenty-first century. As both wood and fine craftsmanship become more precious in a machine-made world, the art not only reminds us of a simpler past, but it also shows nothing is fixed and old skills can evolve unexpectedly. The artists in this book acknowledge their predecessors, both ancient and more recent. In turn, we hope the work in these pages will inspire others to grow in new directions.

—TERRY MARTIN, BRISBANE, AUSTRALIA, AND KEVIN WALLACE, LOS ANGELES, CALIFORNIA

MARILYN CAMPBELL

Marilyn Campbell taught herself to turn from a book and found working on the lathe offered numerous creative possibilities, within the limits imposed by the machine. Her highly original combination of wood and epoxy, both as a binding agent and a sculptural medium, allows her to create unique vessels that defy the limits of the traditional wooden form. In her work, it is not always easy to tell what is wood and what is plastic, nor is it easy to detect the lathe's circular argument in the final form.

I see the vessels as representing those grand social events set back in an era when elegance and style were the cultural ideal. I want the viewer to think of fine dinner parties, tuxes and tails, top hats and formal gowns.

Artist Profile

Marilyn earned a degree in anthropology but when, with her future husband, she built a 36-foot sailboat to see the world, she launched herself to a career in woodturning in 1980; self-taught, she was inspired by Stephen Hogbin and Binh Pho.

Studio location: Kincardine, Canada

marilyncampbell.ca

Full Regalia, 2006, holly, epoxy, cherry, purpleheart, paint; 9¾" high x 9½" long x 3" wide. Campbell says, "Full Regalia, being very formal and somewhat austere, echoes the pomp and pageantry of a royal parade."

Come Here Often? 2007, holly, epoxy, paint, curly maple, purpleheart, dye; 9" high x 7¾" long x 2½" wide. Campbell says, "*Come Here Often?* brings to mind a slightly inebriated gent in formal attire trying that age-old line."

Celebration, 2006, holly, epoxy, cherry, purpleheart, paint; 8½" high x 8½" long x 2¾" wide. "In keeping with my theme of high-society decadence, I wanted to give this piece a mood of music and motion," Campbell says. "A celebration of life's good times."

Persuasion, 2006, holly, epoxy, cherry, purpleheart, epoxy, fiberglass, paint; 7⅝" high x 8" long x 2½" wide.

VIRGINIA DOTSON

Woodturning gives Virginia Dotson the opportunity to explore stack-laminating techniques, while its limited scale allows her to develop a concept by working quickly through ideas. She likes to imitate the natural layering of wood grain in her laminated plywood projects. The layers remind her of the sedimentary rock landscapes in the deserts she often visits.

I find interesting interactions between the wood figure and the patterns I have created by layering different woods together. My laminated wood vessels are an expression of the landscape.

Artist Profile

b. 1943 Newton, Massachusetts

Raised in a family of musicians, Virginia studied art at Arizona State University, where she encountered woodturning as an art form; she took early inspiration from Wendell Castle, Bob Stocksdale, and Rudy Osolnik; began her woodworking career as furniture maker before turning to fine art.

Studio location: Scottsdale, Arizona

Sunlight Series #22, 2004. Curly birch and ebonized walnut, 9¼" high x 7¼" diameter. Dotson says the layers of wood echo "layered forms I have observed in nature, like the sedimentary rock landscapes common in the Southwestern United States where I live. Their history is recorded among the layers."

Spiral Vessels, 2001. Italian poplar plywood, graphite; 9" high x 10¾" wide x 15½" deep. Just as a calligraphic brush stroke can contain an entire concept through gesture, Dotson uses form to capture experience and movement.

After Image, 2003. Baltic birch plywood; 7¾" high x 10¾" wide x 13½" deep. Says Dotson, "Animation and beauty may be found in the coexistence of opposites: positive and negative, light and dark, form and space."

Crosswinds, 1990. Wenge, maple;
6¼" high x 16¼" diameter;
permanent collection, Los Angeles
County Museum of Art.

HARVEY FEIN

An inventor and machinist by training and temperament, Harvey Fein starts with an idea for a project then moves on to drafting the shape of it on paper and determining the best jig setup to accomplish it. For his complex designs to succeed, the wood must be bone-dry and tight-grained, which is why he tends to work with kiln-dried tropical hardwoods. He has also modified his Stubby 1000 lathe with a variety of jigs, auxiliary tools, and extensions to make exquisite final pieces.

The feel, the smell, the dust, the chips, the oil, the wax, sanding, shaping—everything about wood appeals to me.

Artist Profile

Harvey got into woodturning in the late 1990s after being gifted a home-turned bowl by a friend; inspired by David Ellsworth and Leon Lacoursiere, he has pursued his hobby alongside his career as co-owner of a window shade business based in New York City.

Studio location: Northwestern New Jersey

www.harveyfein.net

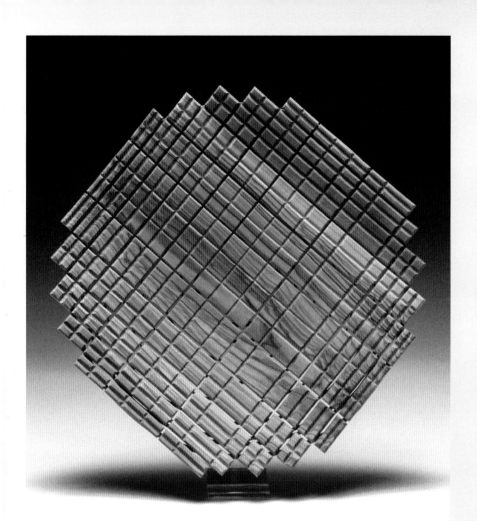

Untitled, 2007. Olive; 1½" high x 15½" wide x 15½" deep. "When I opened up this piece of olive, the linearity of the grain, along with the dark edge, suggested squares. I have done large squares and this was an extension of the idea. Gradation and irregularity."

Untitled Platter, 2006. Jarrah burl, maple burl; 1¾" deep x 18" diameter. "I love the combination of spirals and wild burls," Fein says. "The movement of the spirals and the wildness of the burl create a perfect foil for each other. In this case, the lightness of the maple burl optically enhances the effect of the spiral."

Untitled Platter, 2007. Bubinga, coolabah burl; 2½" deep x 19" diameter. "This piece was drawn out to feature a round piece of coolabah burl I had. The thickness and uniformity of the blank was a great foil for the burl."

4 Points, 2006. Claro walnut,
1¾" high x 17½" wide x 17½" deep.
"*Four Points* started out as an
experiment in vanishing points. Each
set of six lines has a common point
some 28 inches off the center, with
the piece rotated to produce the
pattern and four vanishing points. The
diagonal line of light wood in the claro
walnut is perfectly sited."

J. PAUL FENNELL

J. Paul Fennel prefers to use locally harvested wood species that are not native to the Sonoran Desert environment where he lives, avoiding buying commercially. Working with nature scenery, he creates his patterns by scanning images onto vinyl film. The challenge of woodturning that he enjoys is shaping a two-dimensional image into a three-dimensional vessel form.

The idea is to allow the rhythm of the pattern to express a theme or concept as it traverses the surface, in a visual and tactile language everyone can understand.

Artist Profile

b. Beverley, Massachusetts

J. Paul grew up spending time in his father's workshop and, during school, enjoyed wood shop classes; he earned a BS in engineering from The Ohio State University and an MS degree in engineering from USC before working on the Apollo space program; he was introduced to woodturning in a continuing ed class in 1971.

Studio location: Scottsdale, Arizona

www.jpaulfennell.com

Metallica Green,
1994. Citrus
wood, metal leaf,
lacquer; 8½" high
x 5½" diameter.
In the mid-1990s,
Fennell developed
his interest in
surface decoration
by applying
metal leaf and
lacquer on crisply
turned wooden
vessels. His
current interest
is in pierced and
carved pieces.

View from the Bamboo Garden, 2006. African sumac; 11" high x 7" diameter. Fennell says, "I am fascinated with window lattice patterns typically found in China. In *View from the Bamboo Garden*, I employ a specific pattern—called ice ray or cracked ice—in a theme focusing on the importance of gardens in everyday life, places for solitary or social contemplation of nature."

View from the Garden, 2006. African sumac, 7½" high x 6½" diameter. Fennell has portrayed a garden theme using three elements: the lattice, a textured wall, and the structure of tree branches. Each element is on a different level—the outermost is the tree, the next is the garden wall, the next is the lattice frame, and finally the lattice itself.

De la Mer, 2007. African sumac, 9" high x 11¼" diameter. Carved and pierced, *De la Mer* is inspired by ocean waves and reflected light patterns on the ocean bottom, "from childhood memories when I lived on the East Coast, where the Atlantic Ocean was virtually the front yard of my home, Fennell says.

Leaf Form, 2005. African sumac; 8" high x 8" diameter. "I was fascinated as a youngster to watch beetles skeletonize leaves, leaving only the veins intact," Fennell says. "The background has to be relieved to achieve the effect of raised leaf veins, and the piercing mimics the beetles' handiwork."

Subtlety, 1991. Bleached box elder, 9" high x 5½" diameter. Fennell's early work emphasized the natural beauty of the wood and the created beauty of the turned form, without carving and piercing.

RON FLEMING

In 1984, Ron Fleming purchased an old incinerator on the outskirts of Tulsa and converted it into a home and studio he called Hearthstone, and there he created his masterpieces for over 30 years. His inspiration is the natural world and most of his ideas come from seeing a particular plant, tree, bird, or animal that interests him. He then transforms and stylizes the images, working out the designs in sketchbooks. It can take months for him to finish a single piece.

It is about how I can use the lathe to establish a blank to carve on. You always must have a beautiful form with which to work.

Artist Profile

b. 1937 Oklahoma City, Oklahoma

Ron Fleming grew up in Oklahoma where he spent a lot of time in the workshop of his grandfather, who encouraged him to become an artist; his successful career in commercial illustration allowed him to save enough money to become a full-time woodturning artist in the late 1980s.

Studio location: Boyd, Texas

African Fern Basket, 2004. Redwood; 14" high x 13" diameter. The wild ferns that grow in the hippo trails of the Okavango Delta of Western Botswana inspired *African Fern Basket.*

Athena, 2004. Pink ivory; 10" high x 7" diameter. Athena was inspired by the leaves of the *Phalaenopsis mania* orchid.

Echinacea,
1992. Dogwood
burl and maple;
12½" high x
8½" diameter.
Fleming was
admiring
coneflowers
growing in his
garden when
the idea for
this piece came
to him.

The Guardian,
2005. Walnut with
copper patina;
38½" high x
14" diameter.
The head of the
mythological
griffin and the
body texture of the
African crocodile
inspired Fleming
to create a very
large piece.

New Beginnings, 2003. Redwood burl; 11" high x 18" diameter. *Like African Fern Basket, New Beginnings* is derived from the wild ferns of Botswana.

Spongula, 2001. Bleached madrone; 11½" high x 11" diameter. The giant vase sponge inspired *Spongula*. Fleming used madrone (arbutus) burl, which warps and twists, to create the misshapen form.

LIAM FLYNN

Liam Flynn was a modern master of the neo-classical wooden vessel. His use of plain wood, usually blackened, meant that his shapes had to be perfect, and he succeeded. He used traditional oak, wet and unseasoned, from his native Irish countryside, designing a piece while it was still part of the log. His finished work, ebonized with a solution of acetic acid and iron filings, retains a deep patina that evokes ancient vessels blackened by their long slumber in the peat bog of archaeological sites.

I like to work with green oak. I find the wood to be alive while I'm working it, really responsive.

Artist Profile

b. 1969 Abbeyfeale, Ireland **d**. 2017

Third generation to work in his shop; began woodturning career in the early 1980s after exposure to the work of John Makepeace, Richard Raffan, and others.

Untitled, 2006, Fumed oak; 7½" high x 10" diameter. Fuming with ammonia gives the piece its soft brown color, while allowing the rays in the wood to flash across the carved flutes.

Untitled, 2006. Ebonized oak; 5" high x
9" diameter. The turned form is symmetrical but
the surface carving is offset, giving the ebonized
piece of oak a distinct character.

Still Life with Holly, 2007. Holly; 13½" wide. The
delicately flaring bowl contrasts with the enclosed
form of its partner vessel. One is filled with light,
the other with shadow.

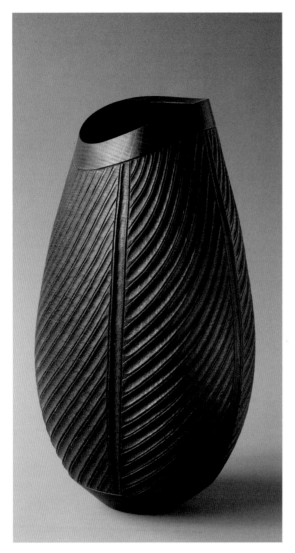
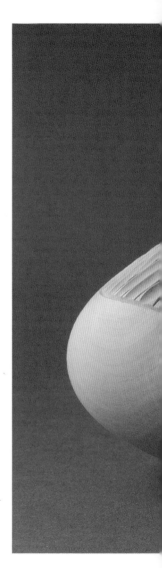

Untitled, 2006. Ebonized oak; 13" high x 7½" diameter.

Untitled, 2006. Holly; 6" diameter.

MARK GARDNER

Early in his career, Mark Gardner made the decision to create a sense of formality with his vessels. His work soon came to be a clear statement of non-function, even when its roots were clearly based on turned bowls, and retains some references to functionality. There is a kind of serene simplicity that allows his pieces to work well when displayed in a ceremonial setting.

I like that the material differs from species to species and tree to tree, which presents new challenges and opportunities.

Artist Profile

b. 1973 Cincinnati, Ohio

Mark started making Shaker furniture at age 16; he earned his BFA in theater design and production from the University of Cincinnati, where his father, a hobbyist woodworker, taught English; inspired by Clay Foster, Kristina Madsen, and John Jordan, he pursued fine art woodturning.

Studio location: Saluda, North Carolina

markgardnerstudio.com

Square Bowl, 2004. Walnut, milk paint; 2½" x 6" x 6". Gardner enjoys the contradiction of producing a square form on the lathe. He turns the top grooves on the spinning block, extending them into space where the wood ends. He enhances the visual contradiction by picking up the turned grooves in the top surface and flowing them over square edges.

Offering Bowl, 2004. Maple, paint; 4" x 32" x 12". The circular lines clearly show *Offering Bowl* was turned on the lathe. It appears the dovetails and raised portions were in the wood when it was turned, but it is a fine illusion because Gardner added them afterward.

Boat Form, 2006.
Cherry, paint; 7" x 34" x
4". Mounted on its own
wall stand, it is not
immediately obvious
that *Boat Form* was
turned at all. However,
the incised grooves
on the underside were
unmistakably made of
the lathe.

Untitled Vessel, 2002. Ebonized maple; 8" x 5" diameter. The incised carving was inspired by Gardner's study of African and Oceanic artifacts in museums and books. He says he is "drawn to the rhythm of repeated carved patterns on ceremonial and utilitarian objects."

Tea Set, 2000. Ebonized ash; 7" x 3" x 11". Working with a large piece of wood, Gardner turns the vessel in the center of a wide disk of wood. Then, he saws most of the disk away, leaving just enough for the handles.

African Blackwood Bowl, 2000. African blackwood; 3" x 3" x 4". *African Blackwood Bowl*, a handled bowl with a delicately sawn strip that connects the handles, is a fine example of Gardner's early work.

Maple Boxes, 1996. Bleached maple; 3" x 2" diameter. Gardner's early work included conventional lidded boxes like this little pair.

DEWEY GARRETT

A lifelong engineer, Dewey Garret has always been eager to face technical challenges. In the early 1980s, drawing on his family's pedigree, this eagerness led him beyond simple furniture making to ornamental woodturning. His calling card technique is to use lamination and negative space to create sculptural vessels. Design and problem solving are an important part of his creative process; after all, he builds his own shop machines and even writes the software to control them.

The mind can envision so much and I can't possibly follow every idea, so the lathe places a limit, yet still offers seemingly endless possibilities.

Artist Profile

b. Richmond, Missouri

Dewey was born to furniture-maker parents; his mother specialized in turning table and chair legs as well as lamps, bowls, and wall sconces; he earned a bachelor's degree in engineering from Northwestern University and a master's from UCLA while working in the aircraft industry in California, eventually working on laser projects at the Lawrence Livermore National Laboratory; inspired by Robyn Horn, he began turning bowls in 1983.

Studio location: Livermore, California

www.deweygarrett.com

Stories, 2005. Ebonized oak, metalized acrylics, patinas; 14½" high x 13½" diameter. "*Stories* is made of turned segments aged with patinas and situated by levels on a tower," Garrett says. "The levels— stories—suggest an unfinished construction of unknown purpose, started and abandoned."

Analysis #1, 1992. Alder and padauk; 3½" high x 12" diameter. Garrett experimented with numerous alternative designs investigating the effects of combining the open forms with their solid counterparts.

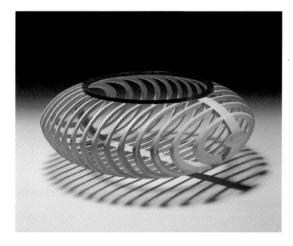

Exploration, 1992. Maple & padauk; 4" high x 14" diameter. Garrett learned a great deal making these forms, and once done he also discovered the moiré effect of apparent motion, to a moving viewer, of an unmoving object.

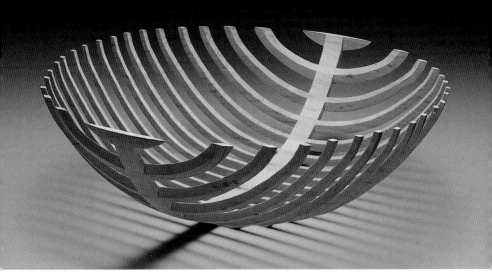

LIM #3, 1993. Bleached maple, padauk; 4" high x 12" diameter. Garrett's explorations led to works with no rim and only a skeleton framework remaining. "I named these LIM, from the idea that less is more expressed by Mies van der Rohe," Garrett notes. "After that, I decided I was finished with the series."

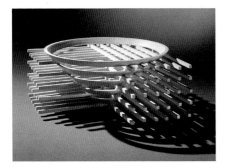

Gridded Cone. Bleached oak, 7" high x 14" wide x 14" deep. In *Gridded Cone*, Garrett placed the remnants of the bowl form at the center of wooden slats. The view changes as the observer moves around the piece.

Visitors, 1996. Ebonized walnut, 8" high x 8" diameter. The intricate pieces are built up with an interior design and then turned to a sphere, carved, and opened to reveal the structure inside.

Impact Grid, 2006. Bleached oak; 11½" high x 11½" wide x 4" diameter.
"In these pieces, I've continued my exploration of bowl forms embedded
in a block but tried to make a stronger effect with the larger block
components," Garrett says.

Palm Vessel with Beads, 2006. Dyed palm; 13" diameter. One winter when it was too cold to turn, Garrett experimented with beads to highlight and intensify the simple carvings in the palm wood.

Pitted Palm Bowl, 2006. Dyed palm; 3¼" high x 13¼" diameter. After turning about a thousand pounds of palm wood, I began to experiment with simple carvings using a rotary burr," Garrett says. "I liked the way the spherical cuts interact with the fibers of the wood."

White City, 2006. Bleached oak; 6" high x 14" diameter. Garrett assembled *White City,* and others in his City series, from many small turned, sawn, and drilled blocks of wood. Bleaching the oak de-emphasizes the wood figure.

LOUISE HIBBERT

Louise Hibbert takes her inspiration from her fascination with marine life, whose microscopic creatures, plants, and fossils give her an incredibly fruitful bank of shapes and forms to translate into wood. After researching a particular life form whose shape she wishes to create, she draws the project to scale. She likes wood as a medium because it lends itself to an organic flow of lines and sharp details. With a jeweler's saw, pyrography machine, paint and polyester resin, in addition to her vintage lathe, she brings fascinating, lifelike forms out of the wood.

Having been alive, wood has a warmth that resonates with my designs. It is important to me that people are able to sense this quality when they interact with my pieces.

Artist Profile

b. 1972 Southampton, England

Louise grew up by the shores of southern England and is motivated by an ethic of sustainability; she earned a degree in three-dimensional design from University of Brighton; her preferred tool is her beloved 1950 Wadkin Bursgren lathe.

Studio location: Llanfairfechan, Wales

www.louisehibbert.com

Radiolarian Vessel VII, 2004. English sycamore, silver, texture paste, acrylic inks; 6" wide. "*Radiolarian Vessel VII* evolved from an electron microscope image of a radiolarian, a type of zooplankton found throughout the oceans," Hibbert says. "Through the series they started to take on some crab-like characteristics."

Peplus Box, 2007. English sycamore, silver, acrylic inks; 3" long. "I love the undulating surface of the English euphorbia seed that inspired *Peplus Box*," Hibbert says. "Its size allows it to fit snugly in your hand when closed."

Dicoryne Box, collaboration with Sarah Parker-Eaton, 2005. English sycamore, western Australian myall, silver, gold texture paste, acrylic inks; 6½" long. "*Dicroryne conferta*, the main inspiration behind this box, is a hydroid—part of a group of exquisite marine animals," Hibbert explains. "The silver spines on its edges represent the cilia that propel it through the sea." The small scale of the piece encourages handling and the spines require the same careful handling as the small creature might. The magnets holding the box together give *Dicoryne Box* a little extra life when the box snaps closed.

Heuchera Box, 2007. English sycamore, copper, texture paste, acrylic inks; 3½" long. *Heuchera Box* incorporates the range of techniques Hibbert uses in her work, including carving, airbrushing, resin spines, pyrography, metalwork and hidden magnets.

Corymbia, collaboration with Sarah Parker-Eaton, 2004. Maple, silver, gold, acrylic inks. 5" wide. "The barrel-shaped woody pods of the *Corymbia ficifolia*, or red flowering gum, inspired Corymbia," Hibbert says. "For me, the magnificent gum trees are an icon of the Australian landscape."

Thomasia, collaboration with Sarah Parker-Eaton, 2004. English sycamore, silver, gold, texture paste, acrylic inks; 6" high. The ovary of *Thomasia foliosa*, with an outer surface covered with short, dense, star-like hairs, inspired *Thomasia*. The *Thomasia foliosa* woodland shrub grows in Western Australia.

Rumex, collaboration with Sarah Parker-Eaton, 2004. English sycamore, silver, texture paste, acrylic inks; 4½" wide. Part of the Genus Australis series, this dark, textured fruit capsule, with its hooked teeth, opens to reveal a vibrantly colored treasure within.

MICHAEL HOSALUK

Michael Hosaluk, as one of the founders of the Emma Lake Collaboration, has played an enormous role in community building for woodturning artists practicing their craft in disparate places around the globe. He cherishes the positive effects that networking with other makers has had on his own work, not to mention his own life. Although primarily interested in the medium of wood and the lathe, his projects often take on a life of their own, demanding alternative materials, techniques, and tools, and he happily follows his genius.

It's our ideas that are most important, not the material.
Craft doesn't only deal with aesthetics, but also with our social
and ideological lives.

Artist Profile

b. 1954 Invermay, Canada

Michael grew up on a farm in Saskatchewan where mother knitted and father made furniture; he began cabinetmaking career immediately after high school then shifted to fine art woodworking in the 1970s, eventually helping to establish the world-renowned Emma Lake Collaboration in the 1990s.

Studio location: Saskatoon, Canada

www.michaelhosaluk.com

Untitled, 2006. Arbutus (madrone); 10½" high x 10" to 11½" wide. Untitled was turned and carved when the wood was still unseasoned or green, so it has dried oval-shaped.

Bird Vase, 2006. Ash, acrylic airbrush medium, 11" high x 4" diameter. It requires many layers of color to achieve a complex image such as this, and yet vestiges of the wood figure still show through. Collaboration with Laura Hosaluk.

Scribble, 2005. Ash, acrylic airbrush medium; 15" high x 4½" diameter. Hosaluk is a master of finishes. It would be easy to mistake this for the glazing on a fine ceramic pot, but the glimpse of wood in the interior confirms that it is turned wood. With typical nonchalance, Hosaluk has scribbled circles on the surface, at once both casual and careful.

Untitled, 2002. Maple and birch, 4" to 6" high x 2" to 4" wide x 5" to 8" long. A few coats of acrylic paint and the fish are finished.

Birch Bowl, 2006. Birch, birch bark; 3½" high x 6" diameter. Hosaluk has veneered the outside of this bowl with patches of birch bark he harvested near his home, linking the simple bowl back to the tree it came from.

Bowl of Strange Fruit. Maple, 2005. Arbutus, birch, acrylic paint, horse and dog hair; 6" high x 4" deep x 24" long. Hosaluk enjoys collaborations, in this case with 12 other artists.

PETER HROMEK

For Peter Hromek, form takes precedence over the appeal of the visual and tactile qualities of the wood. He specializes in multi-axis pieces that look organic, like cells, or seeds or seedpods. His work seems to defy logic; you can't see how he could have hollowed them out, or what the lathe had to do with it. In fact many people find his pieces so startling they can't quite believe they are made of wood. It is this improbability that makes Hromek's work unique. He has built

on a sound sense of form and line, which made his simple hollow forms work so well, and he has taken it to an entirely different level of sophistication.

I have heard people say my work is sensual. I like that idea.

Artist Profile

b. 1947 Czechoslovakia

In 1969, Peter moved to Germany to study and work in engineering, making jewelry on the side and, while playing bass in a bluegrass band, making high-quality guitars; in 1986 he taught himself woodturning and has been making and exhibiting since.

Studio location: Schwarzenfels, Germany

www.salzundpfeffermuehlen.de

Tripod, 2002.
Maple; 14" high.
An early piece,
Tripod was
turned as three
discrete forms,
which were
then cut at the
rim and glued
together. The
work required
endless trial-
fitting and
adjusting, and
Hromek wanted
to achieve the
same effect in
a single piece
of wood.

Venus #1, 2006. Box alder, partly stained; 16" high. This multi-axis turning, made from one large piece of wood, exemplifies Hromek's work. Deceptively, the three lobes were each hollowed out from what has become their bottom ends. The opening at the top was partially formed on the lathe, and partially carved.

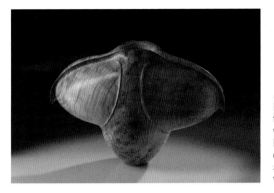

Small heaven #1, 2005. Sugar maple burl; 15" wide. *Small heaven #1,* turned on three axes, leaves the viewer wondering how it could have been hollowed on a lathe. Hromek did much of the hollowing through the openings at the ends of the lobes, not through the vessel's mouth.

Submarine, 2005. Sugar maple burl; 15" long. Perhaps the simplest of Hromek's logic-beaters, it should not be possible to turn a piece like *Submarine* on the lathe. To imagine how it was done, it is necessary to see it partly as a spindle turning, partly as a vessel, and partly as a carving.

Venus #2, 2004. Alder, 16" diameter. *Venus #2* emphasizes the sensual curves that so please the maker.

Spindle, 2006. Ebonized robinia; 13" long. There is
a serenity about *Spindle*. It is simply a conventional
vessel cleverly cut to show grain in unexpected ways
and then laid down in repose.

Small Heaven #2, 2003. Stained cherry; 16" wide.
Hromek has plugged the openings in the ends of the
lobes, leaving no trace of how the form was hollowed
out. The ebonized exterior contrasts wonderfully with
the rich wood texture of the interior.

Paradise, 2007. Maple; 13" high.

STEVEN KENNARD

Steven Kennard's work combines woodturning, carving, and the creation of interesting surface textures. He is inspired by textures he sees in the natural world and his surface texturing techniques have developed from an impulse to create visual and tactile illusions, which he first developed as a theater set designer in the 1970s. He uses the lathe as the jumping-off point for his sculptures; for texturing, he employs a flexible-shaft tool with a variety of burrs, using an optical visor to view the fine detailing.

I am not preoccupied with what is the "right way" or "wrong way" to do something, providing I can achieve what I want. My focus is on the final work.

Artist Profile

b. 1956 Enfield, England

Steven started out making furniture and restoring antiques in Suffolk, England in the 1970s and then designing stage sets for theater; inspired by David Pye and Stephen Hogbin, he turned to fine art sculpture in wood; he moved to France in 1989 and began exhibiting work; moved in 1997 to Nova Scotia.

Studio location: Canning, Canada

www.stevenkennard.com

Spiderman, 2007. African blackwood, French boxwood; 4¼" high x 3¾" diameter. The spiderweb decoration Kennard engraved into the surface grew from the comic book character.

Lost Orchard, 2007. African blackwood, cocobolo, thuya, ivory; 2½" high x 3⅛" diameter. *Lost Orchard* was inspired by the old apple orchards in the Annapolis Valley, Nova Scotia, where the artist lives: "Their stark appearance against the winter landscape will be sadly mourned as these are being decimated around us."

Lacey Sputnic, 2007. African blackwood, cocobolo, 3" high x 3" diameter. "The form of *Lacey Sputnic* was inspired by the capsule carrying the astronauts that parachuted into the ocean from space exploration in the early days," Kennard says.

RON LAYPORT

Ron Layport interprets the natural world in the language employed by ancient cultures, but seen through the lens of contemporary art and design. Using animal effigies combined with vessel forms, he clarifies the connection between contemporary wood art and approaches employed by humankind for centuries. An ecologically minded artist, he prefers domestic woods sourced locally; his favorites are maple, cherry, and

especially sycamore. For his larger vessels he uses the full diameter of a log, turning into end-grain, whereas for bowls he turns directly from the split log, untrimmed. Post-lathe, his sculpting process involves rotary tools and many other tools at hand, and can take up to six weeks.

I approach it like a canvas. Even though I know what I am hoping to achieve, I try to be receptive to opportunities and changes of direction as they present themselves. The piece continues to evolve like a painting.

Artist Profile

b. Elyria, Ohio

When computerization turned Ron away from a long career in advertising in the 1980s, he began making high-quality furniture; after taking a workshop with David Ellsworth in 1992, he turned to fine art woodworking, which he has pursued as a full-time profession since the early 2000s.

Studio location: Pittsburgh, Pennsylvania

Spirit Whites (On Sky Blue Pale), 2006. Maple, turned, sculpted, bleached, pigmented; 10¼" high x 9" diameter. In creating *Spirit Whites*, Layport perfected the turned form, then reduced it to a nearly weightless object that defies, yet defines, the power of negative space. "To witness a gathering of spirits, on a blissful summer's afternoon, is to understand the mystical nature of this vessel," Layport says.

Silk Morning, 2005. Maple, turned, sculpted, bleached, pigmented; 14½" high x 8½" diameter. "I wanted to achieve fluid motion and a sense of depth within the parameters of the vessel form. I sought rhythm and oneness, a continuum of elements, each flowing to the next. The mystery and wonder of an eco-system, perfected in the morning whiteness."

Incarnation of the Salmon King, 2006. Sycamore, ebony, brass, copper wire, pigment, dye; 14¼" high x 11" wide x 7" deep. Part of a series—Vessels from a Distant Dance—exploring the turned vessel form as a ceremonial or life mask. Layport uses wood and space to create a segmented effect. Stylized ebony fins support the object and create a sense of motion and mystery.

MIKE LEE

The wood sculptures of Michael Lee harmonize form, gesture, and texture with abstract forms inspired by his experience of nature. He begins working on a new piece with a sense of the shape, but relies largely upon intuition as the work develops, relishing the unpredictability of wood as a medium. The sculptural forms that result from the process make it clear how much his natural environment—his favorite surfing beach is ten minutes from his studio—  affects his work. While developing a piece, Lee cradles it his hands, turning it over and examining it as it evolves. Lee tends to work on a scale conducive to the process, which provides a sense of intimacy and results in tactile and visually seductive work.

A lot of it is intuitive. Often a couple of hours will fly by and I'll look down at the piece and not even know how I got there.

Artist Profile

b. Oahu, Hawaii

Inspired by surfing, the stories of Stephen King, and memories of pieces of carved art his mother brought back from China, Mike taught himself woodturning to escape the boredom of a job in computers; after attending the Arrowmount School of Arts in Crafts in the early 1990s, he made woodturning his full-time career.

Studio location: Oahu, Hawaii

www.leewoodart.com

Our House, 2005. Kamani, kingwood, yellowheart, padauk, Gabon ebony, lignum vitae; 6½" long x 11" wide x 10½" deep. "*Our House* is a family portrait in which our *Ohana* is nestled in their humble abode," Lee says. "Our house always has been a place of refuge and comfort for me and my family."

Celestial Seasons, 2005. Koa, gabon ebony, padauk, yellowheart, lignum vitae, various gold leaf, 4½" high x 10" wide x 11" deep. "I wanted to convey the changing of the seasons by using the different colors of wood for the pods and further enhancing them with various shades of gold leaf," Lee says. "The brown tones of the bowl laced with the sapwood clouds represent mother earth cradling her celestial seasons."

Brood, 2005. Cocobolo rosewood, Gabon ebony, tagua nuts, 3½" high x 6" wide x 8" deep. Says Lee, "*Brood* represents my ongoing fascination with family, fossils, and fantasy.

Ohana, 2004. Lignum vitae, milo, Gabon ebony, koa, yellowheart; 4" long x 4" wide x 3½" deep, to 2" long x 2" wide x 1¾" deep. *"Ohana* means family in Hawaiian," Lee says. "The piece is a family portrait representing me, my wife, Debbie, son, Zachary, and daughters, Kassidy and Kaiana."

Object of Our Affection, 2006. Gabon ebony, fine silver, 3" high x 5" wide x 11" deep. "*Object of Our Affection* represents a family portrait of my wife and I, as starfish vessels, cradling our first-born."

ALAIN MAILLAND

Alain Mailland's works defy the imagination, because the forms he produces are largely created on the lathe using unique mounting and turning techniques he has perfected since the early 1990s. His observations of nature inform his designs; as a child he studied the forms of plants and made herbariums with his mother. After turning and carving a new piece, usually in green wood, he lets it dry, monitoring the development of distortions and slowing down the drying process if necessary. When the piece is dry, he carves, sands, textures, sandblasts, and steam-bends the wood into something almost magical. Turning is a magical process that gives a center to the piece and allows you to make hollow forms. Everything in the universe is made with circular elements, from cells and atoms to galaxies.

Artist Profile

b. 1959 Côte d'Ivoire

After moving to Paris at age 4 with his family, Alain became fascinated with Impressionism; he studied art at l'Ecole d'Art de Cergy-Pontoise then worked as a mason, carpenter, and roofer near Paris before, in 1991, moving to the south of France to work as a self-employed carpenter and fine artist in wood.

Studio location: Chamborigaud, France

www.mailland.fr

**The Elegance
of Pelagie.**
2005. Pistachio;
11" high x
8" diameter. The
extraordinary
fluidity of
Mailland's
shapes seem
particularly
well suited to
representing
sea creatures.

Back to the Sea, 2006. Arbutus (madrone) root, 19¾" high x 9" diameter. Mailland had to remount the burl root on the lathe to turn each of the small vase shapes. Each one requires changing the orientation of the wood in relation to the axis of rotation and to its position on the chucking system.

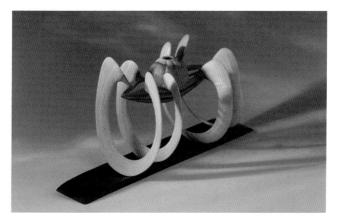

Solar Ship, 2007. Lignum vitae; 6" long x 5" diameter. The circular rims supporting the central vessel were turned on the long axis and their centers were carved away. The piece was rotated 90 degrees and rechucked to turn the central vessel. The boat form under the vessel was wholly carved.

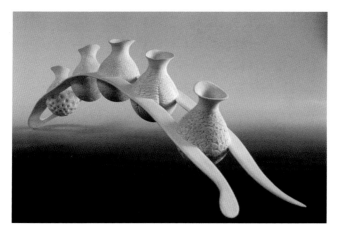

Rainbowls, 2005. Hackberry, 36" x 4" x 9". To make *Rainbowls*, Mailland had to combine multicenter turning, carving, and wood bending.

Eureka, 2003. Hackberry, 21" high x 19½" diameter. It is easy to imagine Mailland struggling to solve the problem of how to make this piece. Its core explodes into flaring petal forms, just like the idea: "Eureka! I have it!"

I Had a Dream, 2006. Arbutus (madrone) root; 5½" diameter. Though it is difficult to determine which parts of the complex piece were turned and which were carved, Mailland maintains the lathe remains the essential center of his work.

Trio, 2004. Pistachio; 11" high x 7¾" diameter. Inverting what we might expect, Mailland makes the bird-mouthed vessels into the base of *Trio*. Are they wings or tails at the top? They can be anything you like. It's hard to believe such a complex form can be turned and carved from a single piece of wood.

THIERRY MARTENON

Thierry Martenon has a genius for producing the unexpected and, consequently, has established himself as one of the most collectible artists in his field. Clearly influenced by his interest in graphic art, his work often looks like sketches solidified, drawn concepts brought to three-dimensional fruition. He uses simple forms, aiming for a degree of serenity; his surface treatments give his pieces extraordinary qualities. While the treatments seem simple, they are the result of meticulous work. Even seemingly brutal tools like the chainsaw, acid, or blowtorch are wielded with great care. He incorporates rustic materials such as copper, stone, linen, tin, or resin in his sculptural pieces.

When I get a good idea, I run to the stock of wood and it starts.
It's like wild dance and until it is complete, all my brain can think
about is that idea.

Artist Profile

b. 1967 Grenoble, France

Inspired by his woodworking fathers and the village woodturner growing up, and then by the work of Jean-Francois Escoulen, Thierry graduated from the Greta Tête d'Or institute to become a cabinetmaker; he became a woodturner in 1998.

Studio location: Entremont-le-Vieux, France

www.thierrymartenon.com

Untitled #21122001,
2001. Maple and
white acrylic;
16" high x 8¾" diameter.
Wonderfully proportioned
and simply decorated,
the form is perfect.

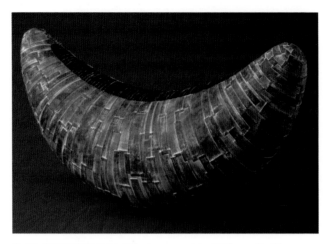

Untitled #27022004, 2004. Walnut, veneer, slate; 16" long x 6" wide x 9" high. This horned vessel embodies all the elements of Martenon's work—an unexpected shape, juxtaposed materials, and superb surface treatment.

Untitled #06012005, 2005. Maple, slate; 19" diameter. Martenon's juxtaposition of two unlikely materials, slate and wood, is typical of his approach. He is unrestricted by conventional expectations.

Untitled #14022004, 2004.
Walnut, elm, veneer, slate;
36" high x 6" diameter.
Patches of veneer give a
remarkable textured effect
to the surface of this
turned form.

Untitled #05052004, 2004. Walnut and slate; 22" long x 6" diameter. *Untitled #05052004* resembles a ceremonial vessel to be held in both hands. The carving on the body reflects the edges of the embedded slate.

MICHAEL MODE

In the early 1990s, Michael Mode's work changed substantially, ranging from miniature chess sets fitted within lidded vessels, to architecturally inspired domed and winged forms reminiscent of the Mughal architecture he had seen long ago, when he lived abroad in India in the early 1970s. The realization of where his inspiration was coming from led

to a series of laminated vessels of colorful and intricate design with seemingly infinite varieties of color and pattern. The patient, meticulous craft tradition of that region inspired him to push himself as an artist.

I began knowing nothing, and was very tentative and private. Today, I have a large amount of confidence in my work, and the wonderful fluidity and fluency of technique makes the creative process very sweet.

Artist Profile

b. 1946 Quakertown, Pennsylvania

Michael attended Haverford College to study creative writing but left in junior year; traveled to Morocco and Kashmir in a two-year tour, absorbing Islamic and Mughal Indian design influences; after moving back home, taught himself woodturning, on a homemade foot-powered lathe, at age 29, then gained experience working for local cabinetmaker, laminating guitar necks; inspired by meeting David Ellsworth, he began exhibiting his own work in galleries in 1982.

Studio location: Bristol, Vermont

www.michaelmode.com

Slow Roll, 2005. Ziricote, wenge, purpleheart, kingwood, pink ivory wood; 6½" high x 11¾" diameter. Often it is simply the beauty of the wood that motivates me," Mode says. "In this case, the ziricote amplified by the color of pink ivory wood and kingwood kept me going."

Zebra Rising, 2004. Wenge, holly, koa; 5¾" high x 8½" diameter. The title of the bowl, an exploration of complexity and serendipity, reflects the black-and-white patterning on a zebra.

Intersections, 1999.
Purpleheart, holly,
wenge, ebony, pink
ivory wood; 11" high x
8½" diameter. " Lidded
vessels were my
primary object from the
beginning of my turning
focus in 1975 until the
spring 1999, when I
became interested in
the stack lamination
process of bowl
making," Mode says.

Of Many Hands, 2005. Wenge, mahogany, pink ivory wood, purpleheart; 9" high x 15¾" diameter. A signature design represents Mode's entire bowl-making period.

Boat of Babel, 2006. Lacewood, holly, whalebone; 8" high x 8" wide x 32" deep. "The pattern reminds me of an Arabic script called kufic, each line of which is stating something different at the same time."

WILLIAM MOORE

A fine arts sculptor by training, William Moore's encounter with Lynn Hull's spun metal works influenced him to think about combining turned wood and spun metal, the two materials he most enjoys working with. Since then, creating sculptures founded on strong relationships between wood and metal elements has driven his career. He makes the turned wood element first, and then develops the spun and/or fabricated metal elements to complement the

wood and make the composition whole. He must complete the two processes separately and once he has created the metal elements, the wood may need to be carved and tweaked to achieve the perfect fit. To fit metal to wood, he turns a solid duplicate from hard maple, onto which he actually spins the metal. The final step before assembly is patination of the metal.

I most enjoy exploring a new idea, and solving the compositional and technical problems.

Artist Profile

William learned woodturning from his mother, who bought a lathe in the early 1950s; inspiration in college came from Henry Moore, Philip Grausman, and Barbara Hepworth; a trained sculptor, he earned an MFA from the University of Michigan in the 1970s.

Studio location: Helvetia, Oregon

Lidded Orb, 2006. Mahogany, ebony, bronze, copper, brass; 10½" high x 11" wide x 12" deep. "Several cut-off pieces of spun metal were the inspiration for *Lidded Orb*," Moore says. "These pieces became the two halves of the hinged lid of a spherical vessel. All I had to do was make it all work."

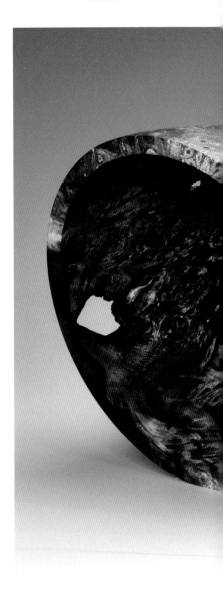

Inverness, 2000. Oak burl, bronze; 10" high x 10" wide x 5" deep. "The metal portions are not decorative additions, but rather are integral to the whole," Moore says. "The body is turned oak burl. Mimicking traditionally styled handles of kitchen cutlery, the wood on either side of the handle's bronze spine are of the same oak. All other elements are bronze. To provide contrast, some bronze elements have a brushed finish. Others have a speckled texture with a brown patina."

Ochoco, 2005. Buckeye burl, copper; 9½" high x 23" wide x 12" deep. "My goal in juxtaposing the two forms was to take them out of the context of being seen as vessels and instead to have them viewed as sculptural forms within a botanical reference," Moore says.

Equilibrium, 2006. Maple burl, copper, bronze; 11⅜" high x 23½" wide x 13¼" deep. Recently, Moore has turned toward exploring gesture and balance to create a sense of movement. He combines multiple-axis hollow forms with spun metal to create a sense of equilibrium, or coming to rest.

Euphrates, 1990. Madrone, copper;
64" high x 17½" wide x 11½" deep. "I
created *Euphrates* when I was interested
in ceremony, ritual, and symbolic
objects," Moore says. "The stand, the
vessel, and its stopper create a totem-like
composition."

ROLLY MUNRO

New Zealand wood artist Rolly Munro's wonderfully textured and enhanced vessels are not only the result of inspired vision, but of considered elements, balanced and complementary. He almost always has a theme in mind before starting a new project; he always knows exactly what he is going to do before he starts cutting. Taking inspiration from his coastal home, he works almost exclusively with marine forms.

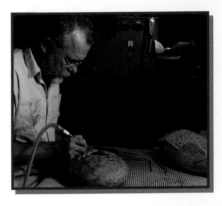

Art forms are a melding of technique, the physical act of making a piece, and expressing the content within a work.

Artist Profile

Early in life, Rolly was turned onto art by an uncle who was an art teacher and sculptor; inspired by Jacob Epstein, Henry Moore, and Barbara Hepworth, he went to art school in the 1970s, where he discovered the lathe; he also has developed his own line of woodturning tools.

Studio location: Wellington, New Zealand

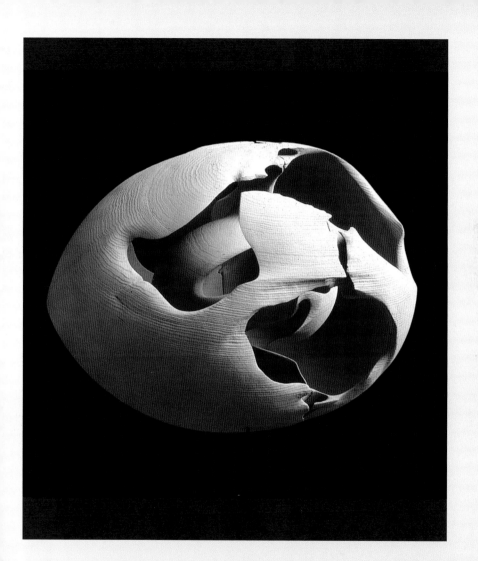

Flotsam, 1990. Kauri wood, turned, carved and sandblasted; 15" wide x 11¾" diameter. Small tongue and groove lock the two hollowed halves together. The sandblasted shapes evoke wind-and-a-sea-scoured shells found on the beach.

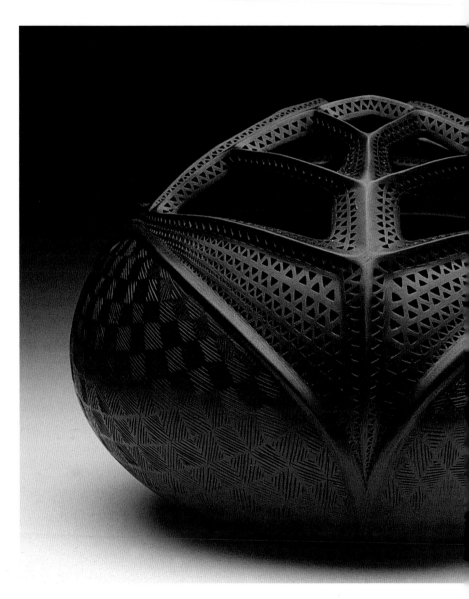

Mahanga Form, 1999. English walnut; 4¼" high x 11" diameter. Says Munro, "It continues the shellfish theme. The palm spikes express clutching tentacles, while the incised design evokes the creature's camouflage of light and water."

PuhaPuha Form, 1999. Ebonized kauri turned and carved; 7¾" high x 11" diameter. The eloquent surface decoration draws on traditional Maori carving. The intense patterns are both incised and pierced. The complex mouth of the vessel, with its intricate carving, is pure Rolly Munro.

The Crow of a Small Amphibious Teapot, 2000. Tawa, English walnut, raspberry jam wood, pink ivory wood; 11¾" high x 7¾" diameter. The idea of the piece itself is astonishing enough, but the detail is even more fascinating. Examining the beautifully carved legs more carefully, it is clear the birdlike feet are partly embedded in the ground, possibly an observation by Munro as his feet scuffed the sand on his daily beach walks.

Refit in Lilliput, 1998. Matai, English oak, western red cedar; ebonized pohutukawa and other woods, glass, copper, cotton; carved, turned, assembled, pigmented, patinated and polished; 16½" long x 39½" high x 11¾" wide. Says Munro, "It's an exciting voyage which I hope arrives at unique destinations."

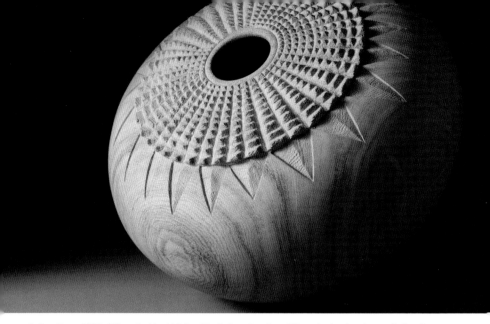

Hollow Form, 1998. Silky oak; 11¾" high x 17½" diameter. One of Munro's simpler pieces, *Hollow Form* still shows his trademark carving. Much of the patterning is indexed and defined on the lathe, then later refined by careful hand carving.

Pattern #12 906 431, 2001. New Zealand kauri; turned, carved and sandblasted; 23½" long x 17½" high x 21½" wide. Resembles whale vertebrae washed up on the beach, or some corroded mechanical part, such as a propeller.

CHRISTOPHE NANCEY

Christophe Nancey's work clearly expresses his empathy with nature. His aim as an artist is to create a symbolic picture of the living process, to create pieces that appear to have been found as they are. Some look like seeds and seed pods while others look like the eroded aftermath of natural events that occurred in the distant past, as he puts it. He tends to use mainly roots and burls, and he embellishes his work with pewter inlay, texturing, and pigments, to create the effects he wants to achieve.

I turn for only ten to twenty percent of the workshop time. Most of the time is spent on carving, texturing, pigmenting, inlaying, finishing. . . . I suppose I have moved beyond simple woodturning and have become a wood artist.

Artist Profile

Christophe started woodworking as a teenager, helping his cabinetmaker father; works from a studio in a 200-year-old stone barn in Burgundy; joined the international community of fine art wood artists in the 1990s through the conferences organized by Jean-Francois Escoulen.

Studio location: Château du Bois, France

www.atelier-nancey.com

Seed, 2006. Heather root, pewter, pigment; turned, carved and textured; 13" diameter. Nancey strives to persuade viewers his sculptures were found just as they are.

Hollow Form, 2001, Manzanita, pewter; 9½" high. *Hollow Form* is reminiscent of the natural-edged work popular in the 1980s, but Nancey has made it his own with the subtle pewter inlay.

The Guardians, 2004. Heather root, pewter, pigments; turned on two axes, carved and textured; heights 7¾" and 9½". The solid forms seem like alien life. It is quite difficult to turn simple shapes like this, because the protruding part has to be turned separately from the main body, before it can be carved.

Fragment, 2004. Manzanita, pewter, pigments; turned and textured; 13½" diameter. Some pieces are like the eroded aftermath of natural events that occurred in the distant past, but which still persist.

Cocoon, 2003. Manzanita, pewter, pigments; turned, carved and textured; 19½" long. Some of Nancey's pieces appear to be natural objects found in an imaginary forest.

Horizon, 2007. Elm burl, pewter, pigments; turned inside, carved and textured; 29½" high. In *Horizon*, Nancey has taken the turned form into the realm of sculpture. As he says: "The main challenge I have to face during a day of work is to be free of the limits of technique so I can focus on finding the best balance and the strongest expression for the piece I'm making."

BINH PHO

Binh Pho told stories with his work and he was one of the few woodturners who focused largely on autobiographical themes. In Pho's work, the difficulties he faced in life were transformed through a unique aesthetic language. A love of color, Eastern imagery, and modern art are obvious in his pieces. While Pho was known as a woodturner, he viewed turning simply as a means of creating forms to express three-dimensional imagery. His three main techniques for surface treatment were airbrushing, piercing/ texturing, and gilding, and when he used them in combination, the results were stunningly beautiful.

As a tree grows, the challenges it faces become part of its character. . . . As an artist, my mission is to reveal the beauty and, in some way, exalt the life record of a once-living organic thing . . . to allow it to live again in a new way.

Artist Profile

b. 1955 Ho Chi Minh City, Vietnam **d**. 2017

Binh fled Communist Vietnam in the late 1970s, eventually settling down in Maple Park, Illinois; meeting Frank Sudol at the Arrowmount School of Arts and Crafts helped give his career focus; takes inspiration from Salvador Dalí and Mihail Chemiakin.

www.binhpho.com

No Way Out, 2007. Citrus wood, acrylic paint and dye; 6" high x 3¾" diameter. *No Way Out* depicts a butterfly trapped in a dense bamboo forest near a stream, based on the story of Pho's capture by the Communists in Vietnam during an escape attempt.

Tears of the Phoenix, 2006. Box elder burl, acrylic paint and dye; 14" high x 7" diameter. The image of the hare appears in the airbrushed color on the right front of the vase form.

Rickshaw Park,
2007. Box elder,
acrylic paint, dye,
gold leaf; 13" high
x 8" diameter.
Pho's father told
him stories of his
childhood, when
the rickshaw puller
would take him
to the park and
then visit with the
other pullers, with
their rickshaws all
lined up.

Dreamer, 2007.
Bradford pear, acrylic
paint, gold leaf;
4½" high x 3" diameter.
Pho often creates
small-scale works,
despite the challenges
involved. "Even in the
small scale of work, all
the details still need to
be there," he explains.
"It is more challenging
to scale down the
detail, working with a
magnifying glass."

Dream of Fire,
2007. Box elder,
acrylic paint,
gold leaf; 5" high
x 2¾" diameter.
Though *Dream of
Fire* is small enough
to cup in your hand,
lush images cover it
on all sides.

GRAEME PRIDDLE

When you look at a Graeme Priddle piece, there is no mistaking who the artist is. Part carved vessel, part patterned burning, part Maori, part environmental statement—the result is work that has a pride of place that is unmistakable. The swirling patterns carved into the wood and the incorporation of seashell into his work are further reflections of the influence of the South Pacific. The Maori extensively use shell in their own work and the patterns Graeme burns into his pieces suggest this tradition. But the most distinctive pieces he makes are his canoe-like forms—compellingly evocative, and as clear a statement of cultural esteem as can be found in any turned work anywhere.

It took many years of frustration producing bowls before I started to find my own voice.

Artist Profile

b. 1960 Lower Hutt, New Zealand

After taking voluntary severance from his job as a radio technician in 1989, Graeme bought a 100-acre bush property and, being introduced to the Whangarei Studio Woodworkers Guild, began a new career in woodturning and living off the land; he takes inspiration from New Zealand's traditional Maori carvers; helped found the biennial CollaboratioNZ art event.

Studio location: Northland, New Zealand

www.graemepriddle.com

Starfish Vessel,
2006. Kauri, mulga,
paua shell, copper;
22½" high x 5½" wide
x 5½" deep. Priddle
explains the series:
"The carved and
textural elements
represent waves that
wash the shore, rock
textures, lichens,
water patterns and the
starfish, driftwood,
and multitudes of
shells left behind by
receding tides. The
apparent fragility
of the vessels also
conveys my concern
our fragile marine
environments are
under constant
threat."

Tahi Rua (One Two), 2007. Matai, acrylic paint; 15" high. Priddle developed the series, which suggests Polynesian canoes, when he was abroad on a residency and was suffering from homesickness. "I wanted to go home, but I didn't want to fly. I kept dreaming about sailing a boat home."

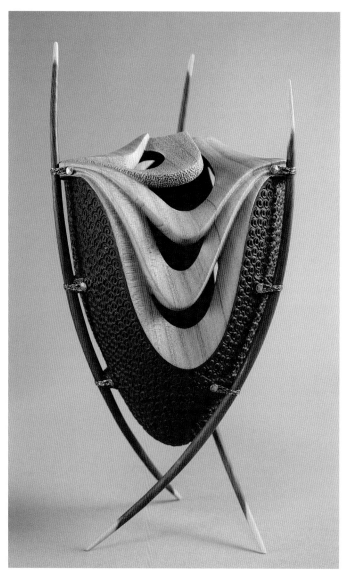

Point Break, 2006.
Monterey cypress,
mulga, copper,
metallic thread;
8½" high x 6" wide
x 3½" deep. Priddle
first became known
internationally
for these carved
vessels, which he
says are inspired by
his interest in the
Pacific environment
and people.

VAUGHN RICHMOND

Vaughn Richmond rarely sketches out his ideas, being gifted enough that he can visualize the finished piece and the steps needed to make it. He prizes flexibility in his artistic process; often he allows inspiration to take over from common sense. He works exclusively in timbers that are unique to his native West Australia, including jarrah and she-oak. Polishing each piece to a striking perfection, he works hard to bring out the rich tones of the woods.

To walk in the forest, admire the beauty of nature, and know I have the potential to reveal the hidden beauty inside a gnarly old log is something special.

Artist Profile

With a father who worked as a woodshop teacher, Vaughn was fortunate to have an early introduction to the craft; he drew inspiration from Art Nouveau, Greg Collins, and Dame Lucie Rie as he began his career in woodturning in the early 1980s.

Landscape, 2003. Jarrah burl, Queensland mountain ash inserts; 13⅜" diameter x 2¾" deep. *Landscape* reflects the scarified Australian landscape. The dots represent the nomadic wanderings of the Aborigines across the land.

Fluted Dish, 2006. Jarrah, pewter, acrylic paints, black coral; 5½" diameter x 1⅝" deep. Fluted platters like this are another of Richmond's signature styles, simple and supremely elegant.

Lightning 1, 2006. Jarrah, acrylic paints; 4" diameter x 2½" high. As with much of Richmond's work, the contrasts emphasize the tones of the wood. The deep, rich tone of the jarrah would not be so obvious by itself, but contrasting it with flat black enhances both the color and figure.

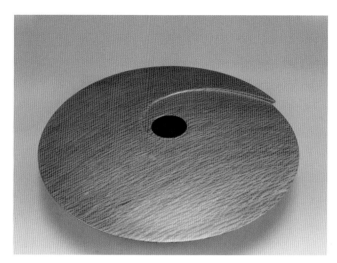

Swisshh, 2005.
Sheoak; 15" diameter
x 3" high. The dynamic
Swisshh is typical of
the earlier designs that
established Richmond's
reputation as a
superb craftsman.

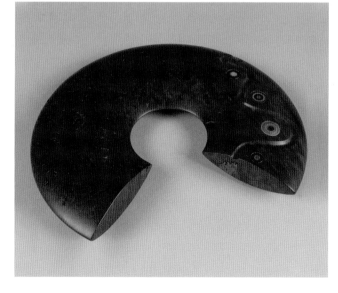

Meeting Place No1,
2006. Jarrah burl,
pewter, acrylic paints;
11¾" diameter x
1⅜" high. In Aboriginal
lore, the winding trail
of the Dreamtime
serpent links sacred
sites. *Meeting Place No1*
echoes the stories.

Dark Sun, 2006. Jarrah, pewter, acrylic paints; 13¼" diameter x 1¾" deep. A hymn of praise to the beauty of the wood, *Dark Sun* highlights its sweep of tones from the dark and richly figured heartwood to the lighter, less mottled sapwood.

Square, 2006. Sheoak; 6" diameter x 2⅜" high. Richmond plays with the idea of the traditional bowl, capping the bowl form with a raised square pattern that is the exact opposite of what we would expect.

Fluted Vase, 2006. Sandalwood, gold leaf, pearl shell, acrylic paints; 5½" high x 2¾" diameter. It requires extreme control to create such fine detail on such a small scale. Richmond creates the fluting on a dedicated system using a swing-arm mounted router. The unfluted section actually emphasizes the fluted areas.

MARC RICOURT

Marc Ricourt's pieces often give the impression of remote cultures or lost civilizations. Indeed, he admits to a fascination with many traditional art forms, from those of Oceania to Africa, and from the Bronze Age to the present. He always works to achieve harmony between the wood, shape, texture, and color of his pieces. He enhances his work with such robust texturing that it is sometimes hard to recognize it was ever turned or even that it is wood. He deeply carves, sometimes incising grooves so far that they break through the walls of the vessel, allowing peep-views of the interior. He makes no attempt to hide the tool marks, but the roughness belies the control required to make such consistent cuts. Often his pieces look wholly organic, with a softness to the finish that makes them appear to be the work of nature. And he does not name his pieces, leaving viewers free to create their own fantastic stories.

The vessel was the first tool created and used by mankind. I find it a wonderful concept—useful, yet mysterious.

Artist Profile

b. 1963 Évreux, France

After mastering cabinetmaking, Marc studied art at the Beaux-Arts school in Dijon; the fortuitous purchase of a used lathe led to his career in wood sculpture; he drew inspiration from Mike Scott, David Ellsworth, David Nash, and Constantin Brancusi, and a visit to the US in 2001 convinced him to pursue woodturning as a career.

Studio location: Vaux-Saules, France

www.marcricourt.errance.net

Vessel, 2006. Scorched elm; 18" high x 12" diameter. It is hard to escape the impression that *Vessel* is corroded cast iron. The surprise comes when you pick up the piece and it is so light.

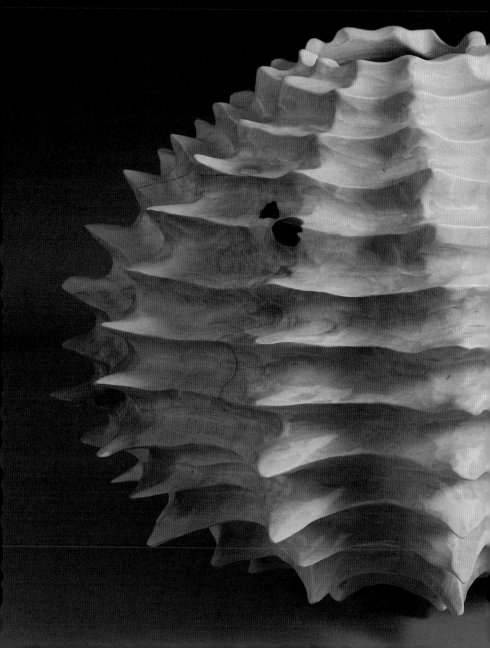

Vessel, 2006. Ash; 18" high x
7½" diameter. In his endless
exploration of the textured surface,
Ricourt contrasts regularity
with roughness, sharpness, and
softness. His pieces trap the light,
creating intriguing shadows.

Vessel, 2006. Pear; 9" high x
11" diameter.

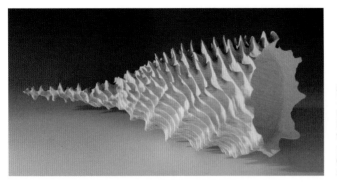

Vessel, 2007. Bleached ash; 25" long x 10" diameter. In a rare departure from Ricourt's upright vases, this reclining piece resembles the carapace of a beached sea creature.

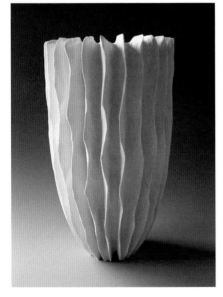

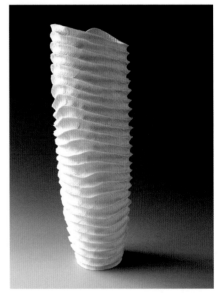

Vessel, 2007. Bleached ash; 17½" high x 10" diameter. The fins on the deeply carved piece approach translucence at the edges, shading the light and softening the whole impression.

Vessel, 2005. Bleached ash; 16" high x 5½" diameter. Inside the deeply carved grooves, the wood grain creates the impression of more carved texture. This piece has an ethereal quality because of the way its bleached hollows catch and reflect light.

Vessel, 2005. Bleached ash; 16" high x 5½" diameter. Inside the deeply carved grooves, the wood grain creates the impression of more carved texture. This piece has an ethereal quality because of the way its bleached hollows catch and reflect light.

BETTY SCARPINO

Betty Scarpino thinks in three dimensions and works intuitively. She almost never plans or draws forms for her work. Her artistic process is like playing; she has patience, and lets the design evolve. The final sanding is where her perfectionist temperament shows. She works methodically and sands by hand until the finish is as silky as she wants. If the result is not

perfect, she is prepared to go back and do it again. The final surface is so well finished that often only a single coat of Danish oil is needed. She retains enough of the evidence of turning in each piece to both acknowledge and deny it is turned work.

I like to discover what lies below the surface, within a turned form. It's like discovering hidden treasure.

Artist Profile

b. 1949 Wenatchee, Washington

Early in life Betty read about the lives of Georgia O'Keeffe, Louise Nevelson, Beatrice Potter, and Barbara Hepworth, becoming inspired toward a life in art; she earned a degree in industrial arts with a focus on woodworking, and later transitioned from production woodworking to fine art wood sculpting.

Studio location: Indianapolis, Indiana

www.bettyscarpino.com

Undercurrent, 2005. Maple, bleach; 13" diameter. Another of the Altered Plate series. Bleaching the wood highlights the deeper natural wood tones of the carved potion.

First Journey, 2005. Ash, stain, liming wax, 44" x 8" x 3". Many of Scarpino's sculptures, in her words, "depict feminine themes, while at the same time, they stand for universal ideas." The only turned elements are the eggs.

Disobedient Currents, 2007. Maple, turned and carved, bleached and painted, stippled, textured; 18" diameter; walnut stand is 15" long. From Scarpino's Altered Plates series. She transforms a turned disc into something very complex, while retaining the simple lines of the original turning.

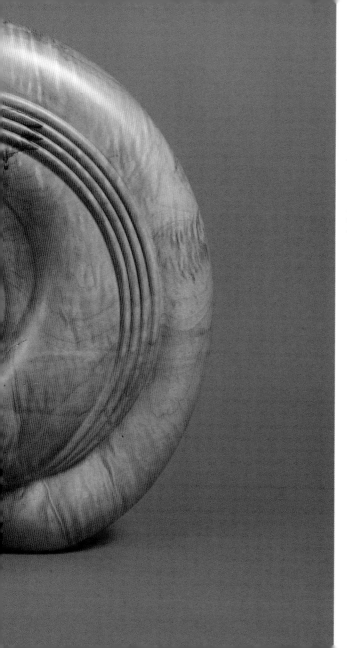

Double Entendre, 2007. Maple, turned, cut, carved, 15" diameter, 3½" thick. *Double Entendre* is a typical example of Scarpino's interactive sculptures. By rearranging the pieces and changing the distance between them, different feelings of closeness, aloofness, dependency, or independence can be evoked. *Double Entendre* was sawn from one turned disk.

NEIL SCOBIE

Neil Scobie's best-known pieces are his Erosion bowls, inspired by the patterns he saw around him in the natural settings around his remote Australian shop. They reflected his memories of eroded gullies from his rural upbringing; while making them, he imagined running water and how it will wear a path through the earth. This series is not only a metaphor for nature, but a clear statement that the old skills, learned through hundreds of years of trial and error, still have a place in the world of wood art. As a teacher, Scobie always stressed the importance of working with the grain. His pieces have a natural feel; they are not arbitrary shapes imposed on the wood.

Artist Profile

b. 1953 New South Wales, Australia **d**. 2016

Influenced by a woodworker grandfather, Neil taught shop in high school for 20 years before, in 1993, becoming a full-time wood artist based in Lower Bucca in his native Australia; he collaborated frequently with his wife, the textile artist Liz Scobie.

Nautilus Bowl, 2006. Huon pine; 9" x 3½".

Nautilus Bowl, 2006. Collaboration with Liz Scobie. Australian red cedar, texture paste, acrylic paint; 6" x 2½". Liz Scobie has partly covered the wood with a finish reminiscent of mother-of-pearl.

Pods, 2007. Rosewood; largest 8½" x 3" x 1½". The pods have been carved after turning, and then partly stippled by burning.

Erosion Forms, 2007. Australian blackwood; 7", 6", and 5" high. Grouping three forms together means they play off each other, enhancing the sense of captured energy.

Land and Sea Series,
2006. Collaboration
with Liz Scobie.
Australian red cedar,
acrylic paint; 9⅜" x
1¼".

DAVID SENGEL

In the late 1990s, David Sengel, widely known for his thorn-embellished sculptures, reassessed his ambitions as an artist. This personal recentering gave him space to think about his work, and he grew determined to make pieces that meant more to him personally, which often means they reflect his fascination with the natural destructive forces in nature. Weathering, bleaching, rusting, and the sculpting by insects are all effects he tries to emulate.

Artist Profile

b. 1951 Radford, Virginia

David learned about woodworking from his father, who kept a shop at home; after studying piano repair in New York he repaired and tuned pianos for more than ten years; in the 1980s he took woodturning classes and, inspired by artists such as Michael Peterson, Andy Goldsworthy, and David Nash, began his career as a fine artist in wood.

Studio location: Boone, North Carolina

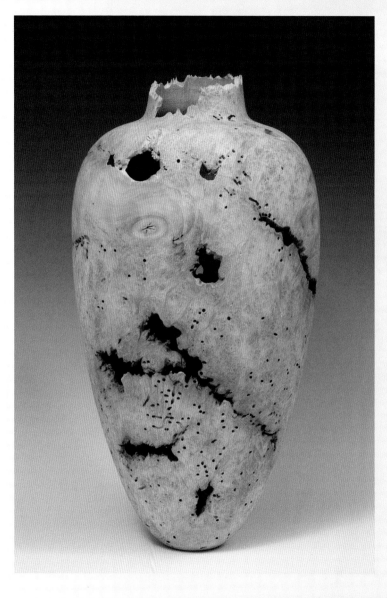

Vessel from the Ocean Floor, 2004. Maple burl; 18" high x 9" diameter.

Sweet Perch,
2007. Spalted maple, various thorns, glass insert; 20" high x 8" wide (excluding the flowers). Sengel combines his love of sculptural turning with his other love, horticulture. The flowers are real, the bird is not, but the bird is no less fascinated by the flowers. The bird's body is mostly turned.

Lidded Vessel, 1996. Dyed maple, locust, and rose thorns; 12" high.

George's Big Plate, 2003. Mountain magnolia; 23" diameter. Sengel is not afraid to make a political comment with his work. He says, "I've longed for the freedom to sit around and make stuff and not care at all what anybody says about it."

Chamber of Woo, 2007. Black walnut, locust thorns; 13" high x 10" wide. The handle is adorned with threatening thorns and serves as a kind of anti-functional statement that fits in well with Sengel's sense of irony.

HAYLEY SMITH

Hayley Smith creates sculptures that marry the turned wood form with geometric fields of color and delicately carved surfaces. She uses color and surface texture created both on and off the lathe in conjunction with the turned form. In her work she eagerly takes up the challenge of finding the balance between the existing character of the wood and what she can add to it. Her work is idea-driven; she works only on one piece at a time, and she spends a great deal of time drawing in her sketchbook and making intricate notes before going to the lathe.

I embraced working three-dimensionally and the subtractive process of woodturning.

Artist Profile

b. 1965 Cardiff, Wales

Hayley encountered woodturning by accident, through trying the lathe in a college arts course; she studied painting and printmaking and earned a BA in arts education.

Studio location: Bisbee, Arizona

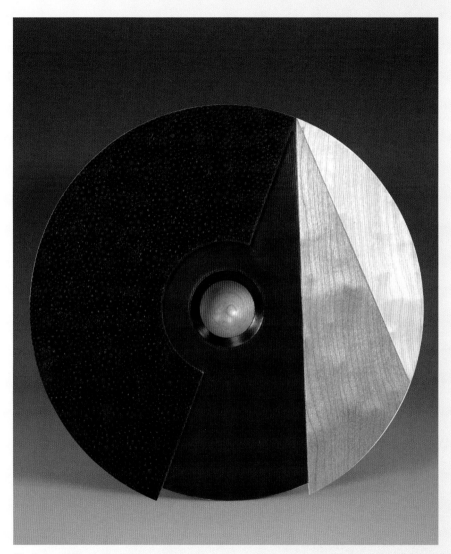

War Dance, 2001. Maple; 1" deep x 9½" diameter. "I had a piece in progress the week of 9/11," Smith says. "It changed and became *War Dance*."

Square Dance VI, 2003. Maple; 1¾" deep x 16¾" diameter. "An exploration of layered squares within circles, and circles within squares," Smith says.

Square Dance III, 2003. Maple, 2½" deep x 17½" diameter. "Sometimes a name leads to a piece, and sometimes a piece leads to a name," Smith says. "Out of all the dances I explored, *Square Dance* led to one piece after another."

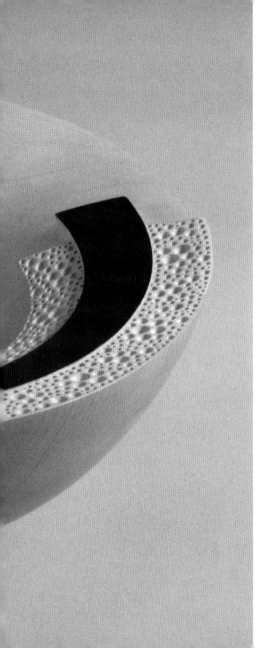

Square Dance VII, 2003. Maple; 2½" deep x 22" diameter. "*Square Dance VII* became the last Square Dance wall piece," Smith says. "The idea behind it was the cliché of a square peg not being able to fit into a round hole, and the small textured square can be seen drifting apart from the round central wood grain bowl."

Hemispherical Bowl #2/99. English sycamore; 3¼" height x 7¼" diameter.

BUTCH SMUTS

Butch Smuts built his woodturning career around the array of woods he collected as an ecologist in South Africa—leadwood, tamboti, wild olive, pink ivory, mopane, and resin tree. His enormous multi-axis bowls posed a serious technical challenge, the solving of which led Butch to develop new artistic features. When a triple-axis bowl is designed well, for example, the point where the three bowls intersect creates a three-faceted sculptural feature. His delicate inlay bowls, produced with the help of a variable speed scroll saw, have garnered for him an international reputation.

The natural feelings of self-expression have to represent an important progression in the career of any artist.

Artist Profile

After taking early retirement from a career in wildlife ecology and environmental management, Butch turned to wood art, following up on boyhood inspiration he received in art class in the early 1960s.

Studio location: Nelspruit, South Africa

Trilobate, 2006. Resin-tree burl; 10" high x 27½" wide. *Trilobate*, a multi-axis turning, began as a very large burl from an African tree, gathered during Smuts' career as a wildlife ecologist. By multi-axis turning Smuts can hollow the inside of the forms on the lathe, but then it is hand-carving to shape the bottom, texture the wood, and finish it.

Dune Landscape II, 2005. Resin tree burl; 6½" high x 27½" wide. To hollow a form like this, Smuts centers each vessel on the lathe.

Out of Africa, 2004. African blackwood, pink ivory, round-leaved kiaat burl inlay; 5½" high x 10⅛" wide. Alongside his large turnings, Smuts also makes delicate little objects such as this vase with a wide rim of thin blackwood and inlays of African motifs.

Avian Menagerie, 2004. African blackwood, pink ivory, round-leaved kiaat burl inlay; 6⅝" high x
12⅛" wide. Smuts finishes his bowls to a fine degree of perfection, "usually down to 800-grit sandpaper
and 0000 steel wool. Then I wipe on a few coats of Danish oil before waxing and polishing by hand."

Nocturnal Surround, 2004. African blackwood, sneezewood, pau marfim inlay; 6½" high x 11⅝" diameter. The intersecting fretsawn teardrop patterns play wonderfully off the circular lathe work.

JACQUES VESERY

When Jacques Vesery stopped looking at wood as a finished product and started seeing it as a canvas, his work grew substantially, and so did his career. As a medium, wood's malleability as a medium suits Jacques, and his greatest pleasure as artist is in painting the surfaces of his pieces.

When someone looks at one of my pieces, they see a basic color. What they might not realize is there are many layers and at least seven different colors that shift across the piece.

Artist Profile

b. 1960 New Milford, New Jersey

Jacques launched his woodturning career in 1985 when, working as a forest ranger in northern New Jersey, he was given an old Oliver lathe, access to a workshop, and free time; he takes inspiration from previous work as a scrimshander in Hawaii and Cape Cod following his time in the Navy as a submariner.

Studio location: Damariscotta, Maine

www.jacquesvesery.com

Traveling Under Watery Skies, 2005-06. Cherry, acrylic; 6" high x 4" diameter. "Although *Traveling Under Watery Skies* appears sculptural, it is based on a classic form,"Vesery says. "By reorienting the form and creating negative space, an illusion occurs, causing the viewer to believe it is from the sea."

A Celadon Sky Dream, 2006. Cherry, gold leaf, acrylic; 5" wide x 2½" deep. "An engaging convergence of color, texture, and proportion in any object forms a unique spirit and soul from birth," Vesery says. "Material and technique then become irrelevant."

Makana Ka Na Hoku (Gift of the Stars), 2006-07. Cherry, gold leaf, acrylic; 5" wide x 2½" deep. While in the Navy, Vesery sailed out of Pearl Harbor. "It is the place, the people and the sea-life of the islands that inspired this piece,"Vesery says. "My connection to Hawaii is still very strong."

Winter's First Sister, from the Pleiades series, 2006. Cherry, maple burl, holly, gold leaf, acrylic; 6" high x 5" diameter. *Winter's First Sister* is the seventh piece of the Pleiades series, inspired by the constellation also known as the Seven Sisters. "The footless form and feather texture convey a sense of deep unknown space for me," Vesery says.

Lorelei's Realm, 1995. Curly maple, Macassar ebony, canarywood; 9½" high x 7" diameter. "In my earlier work, I let material and technique drive what I made," Vesery says. "*Lorelei's Realm* connects to my more recent work. Lorelei's Realm was one of a few pieces that grew from form versus material, though not completely."

L'ecoulement du Ciel Vers La Mer, 2007. Cherry, dyed silver leaf, acrylic, blue fluorite; 4" diameter x 2½" deep. "The sea forms I create are near to my heart, more than anything else I have made,"Vesery says. "I was born in the water sign Aquarius, my native totem is the sea otter, I was on a submarine in the Navy and I have always lived near the sea."

HANS WEISSFLOG

Internationally known for his highly controlled, detailed approaches to woodturning, Hans Weissflog carefully plans and perfectly proportions every piece in advance. He thinks out the steps needed to create the final object. Since he relies exclusively on the lathe to produce his work—he doesn't carve or paint turned work—there is no room for error in his method.

It's a pity nobody collects only my broken pieces, as it would result in large and interesting collections.

Artist Profile

b. 1954 Hönnersum, Germany

Hans studied mechanical engineering and design, becoming a mechanical engineering technician, and, increasingly interested in design, studied woodturning in Hildesheim; his career took shape after viewing the work of Saueracre in a museum; he often collaborates with his son Jakob.

Studio location: Hildesheim, Germany

Twin Tower, 2003.
African blackwood;
14" high x
7½" wide x 2⁹⁄₁₆".
"*The Twin Tower*
shows a seemingly
indestructible piece
of wood, created
by splitting with
an axe, and a very
fragile, turned
part," Weissflog
says. "It is a
combination of
two totally
different kinds of
woodworking."

Saturn Star Bowl, 2006. Putumuju; 2¾" high x 7" diameter. "*Saturn Star Bowl* is the most complicated piece I've ever made," Weissflog says. "You see the star in the ring and the spider pattern in the middle."

Ball Box, 1994. African blackwood, boxwood; 2" high x 2" diameter. *Ball Box* was one of the forms that initially brought Weissflog international recognition. "I often begin with a sphere," he says. "But this time, rather than adding something, I decided to take something away." What he took away was half the material.

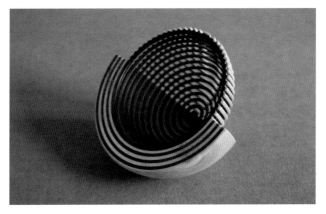

Small Rocking Bowl, 2005. Boxwood, African blackwood; 2½" high x 3¼" wide x 2½" deep. *Small Rocking Bowl* has the same proportions as the large one and is made from two different kinds of wood, offering a contrast in color.

Rocking Bowl, 1996. Cocobolo; 5" high x 6⅝" wide x 5" deep. "With *Rocking Bowl,* I wanted to design a piece with a heavy, massive part that belongs to the earth and a light, pierced-through part to represent heaven,"Weissflog says.

Touching Rings Bowl, 1998. Maple; 2¾" high x 10" diameter. "On the outside of the bowl I cut grooves around different centers," Weissflog says. "All the rings have different sizes, causing the outside rings to touch."

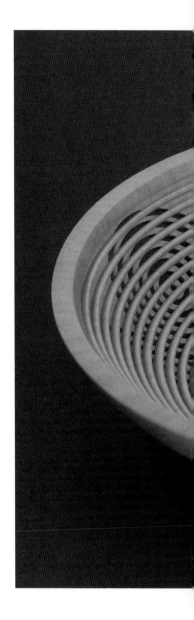

ABOUT THE AUTHORS

Terry Martin is a wood artist, curator, and commentator on wood art. The author of *Wood Dreaming* (1996: Angus & Robertson) and *The Creative Woodturner* (2014: Linden), as well as the former editor-in-chief of the woodturning journal *Turning Points*, he has written hundreds of articles on the subject of wood art. In addition, he has taken part in dozens of wood art exhibitions around the world, and his work is part of many private and public collections devoted to wood art. *terrymartinwoodartist.com*

Kevin Wallace is the director of the Beatrice Wood Center for the Arts in Ojai, California. The author of *Intersection: Art & Life* (2018: Schiffer), as well as numerous other books, he is an independent curator and writer, focusing on contemporary art in craft media (wood, ceramic, and fiber) and wood artists. He has guest-curated numerous exhibitions on the west coast and writes for *American Woodturner* and *Shuttle, Spindle & Dyepot, Craft Arts International* (Australia) and *Woodturning Magazine* (England).

Photo Credits

Cover: courtesy of Michael Mode; pg. ii D. James Dee; pg. iv courtesy of Thierry Martenon; pgs. 12–17 Stephen Simeon; pgs. 18–23 courtesy of Virginia Dotson; pg. 24 courtesy of Harvey Fein; pgs. 25–28 D. James Dee; pgs. 30, 32–35 courtesy of J. Paul Fennell; pg. 31 Abram's Photo/Graphics; pgs. 36–41 courtesy of Ron Fleming; pg. 42 Brendan Leahy; pgs. 43–47 courtesy of Liam Flynn; pg. 48 Nancy Barnett; pgs. 49–52 Tim Barnwell; pg. 53 top and middle courtesy of Mark Gardner; pg. 53 bottom Geoff Carr; pgs. 54–55, 58–59 courtesy of Dewey Garrett; pgs. 56–57 Jim Ferreira; pgs. 60–63 top courtesy of Louise Hibbert; pgs. 63 bottom–65 David Roberts; pg. 66 Jason Hosaluk; pgs. 67–71 Grant Kernan; pgs. 72–77 courtesy of Peter Hromek; pgs. 78–81 courtesy of Steven Kennard; pgs. 82–85 Chuck Fuhrer; pg. 86 courtesy of Mike Lee; pgs 87–91 Hugo de Vries; pgs. 92–97 courtesy of Alain Mailland except for 95 top (Roland Studer); pg. 98 Audrey Martenon; pgs. 99–103 courtesy of Thierry Martenon; pgs. 104–109 courtesy of Michael Mode; pg. 110 David James Clark; pg. 111, 113–114 bottom Dan Kvitka; pg. 112 Harold Wood; pg. 115 courtesy of William Moore; pgs. 116–121 courtesy of Rolly Munro; pgs. 122–123, 125–127 courtesy of Christophe Nancey; pg. 124 Roger Smith; pgs. 128–133 courtesy of Binh Pho; pgs. 134–137 courtesy of Graeme Priddle; pg. 138 Dean Malcolm; pgs. 139, 141–143 Victor France; pg. 140 courtesy of Vaughn Richmond; pgs. 144–149 courtesy of Marc Ricourt; pgs. 150–155 courtesy of Betty Scarpino; pg. 156 Terry Martin; pgs. 157–161 Bob Weeks; pgs. 162–167 Chuck Hearon; pgs. 168, 172 courtesy of Hayley Smith; pg. 169 Charlene Patterson; pg. 170, 173 Cervini Haas Gallery; pg. 171 Maggie Nimkin; pgs. 174–179 Wayne Hayward; pgs. 180–185 courtesy of Jacques Vesery; pgs. 186–191 courtesy of Hans Weissflog; back cover: courtesy of Virginia Dotson (left), courtesy of Liam Flynn (right).